World Map

Atlas 2026

A Visual Journey across the Globe with Detailed Maps, Famous Places, National Flags, Capitals, Landmarks, Population Data, and Essential Geography Facts

NORMA WELLS

This atlas is intended for informational and educational purposes. While every effort has been made to ensure the accuracy of the maps, geographic information, and images contained in this book, the author and publisher make no representations or warranties regarding completeness or accuracy. Geographic boundaries, place names, and statistical data may change over time.

Map data, images, and geographic information are compiled from various publicly available and educational sources.

Published independently.

First Edition: 2026

Author: Norma Wells

ISBN: 9798252316307

Printed in the United States of America

Preface

The world does not stand still. Between the printing of one atlas and the next, borders shift, populations surge, and the names of the places we call home evolve.

The **World Map Atlas 2026** was born from a simple need: clarity. In an era of digital overload, there is still immense value in a physical reference that is easy on the eyes and straightforward in its delivery. This edition has been meticulously updated to reflect the geopolitical reality of 2026—from the inauguration of new capital cities like Nusantara to the latest environmental shifts affecting our coastlines.

My goal in creating this book was to move away from cluttered, hard-to-read maps and instead focus on a clean, high-contrast layout. Whether you are a student, a researcher, or a traveler, I hope this atlas serves as a reliable window into our ever-changing planet.

— **Norma Wells** *March 2026*

About the Author: Norma Wells

Norma Wells is a researcher and author dedicated to making complex information accessible to everyone. With a background in educational publishing and geography, Norma specializes in creating reference materials that prioritize readability and accuracy.

TABLE OF CONTENT

Introduction: How to Use This Atlas in 2026

Welcome to the **World Map Atlas 2026**. Geography is a living subject. As we move through 2026, the way we view our borders, our populations, and our environment continues to evolve. This atlas has been designed as a straightforward, easy-to-read reference guide for students, researchers, and curious minds who want to understand the current state of our planet.

The World in 2026

As of early 2026, the global population has surpassed **8.3 billion people**. This edition reflects the most recent geopolitical shifts, including updated national names and recognized administrative changes. In these pages, you will find:

- **Official Name Updates**: Including **Türkiye** (formerly Turkey), **The Netherlands** (moving away from the "Holland" designation), and **Eswatini** (formerly Swaziland).
- **Updated Capitals**: Accurate listings for all 195 sovereign nations.
- **Climate Data**: 2026 projections for climate zones and environmental shifts.

Navigation and Layout

To make this atlas accessible and "Large Print" friendly, we have organized the content into twelve distinct chapters. Each regional chapter follows a consistent pattern:

1. **Regional Overview**: A high-level look at the continent's geography.
2. **Country Profiles**: Alphabetical listings of nations with their essential statistics.
3. **Quick-Fact Tables**: Bolded data points for easy scanning.

Understanding the Data

Each country profile in this book includes five core metrics:

- **Capital City**: The seat of government.
- **Population (2026 Est.):** Based on the latest United Nations and World Bank data.
- **Official Language(s):** Primary languages used in government and education.
- **Currency**: The national unit of tender.
- **Climate Zone**: The primary weather pattern of the region.

A Note on Maps

This book is designed as a **Reference Atlas**. While it contains essential political and physical maps, it is optimized for clarity and high-contrast reading. If you are looking for specific socioeconomic data or historical context, please refer to the specialized chapters at the end of the book (Chapters 10–12).

Chapter 1: The World at a Glance

This chapter provides a high-level summary of the planet's physical and political layout as of **early 2026**. It serves as the foundation for the regional chapters that follow.

Global Statistics (2026 Estimates)

- **Total Surface Area**: 510.1 million square kilometers.
- **Land Area**: 148.9 million square kilometers (approx. 29%).
- **Water Area**: 361.1 million square kilometers (approx. 71%).
- **World Population: ~8.3 billion people** (passed in early 2026).
- **Total Sovereign States**: 195.
- **Most Populous Continent**: Asia (containing ~60% of the world's people).

Top 10 Most Populous Nations in 2026

Below are the world's population leaders. Note that **India** remains the most populous nation, followed by **China**.

Rank	Country	Estimated Population (2026)
1	India	1.47 Billion
2	China	1.41 Billion
3	United States	349 Million
4	Indonesia	288 Million
5	Pakistan	259 Million
6	Nigeria	242 Million
7	Brazil	213 Million
8	Bangladesh	177 Million
9	Russia	143 Million
10	Ethiopia	138 Million

Major Oceans of the World

The five oceans connect our continents and drive the global climate.

1. **Pacific Ocean:** The largest and deepest ocean.
2. **Atlantic Ocean:** Separates the Americas from Europe and Africa.
3. **Indian Ocean:** Bordered by Africa, Asia, and Australia.
4. **Southern Ocean:** Circles the continent of Antarctica.
5. **Arctic Ocean:** The smallest and shallowest ocean, located at the North Pole.

Geopolitical Snapshot: 2026 Trends

As we enter 2026, several key trends are shaping world maps:

- **Urbanization:** More than 57% of the global population now lives in cities.
- **Environmental Shifts:** Climate change is leading to rising sea levels, particularly impacting low-lying island nations in Oceania.
- **Economic Alliances:** Strategic partnerships for critical minerals and energy are creating new "economic zones" that influence how countries interact.

Key Definition: What is a Sovereign State?

In this atlas, we count **195 sovereign states**. This includes:

- **193 Member States** of the United Nations.
- **2 Observer States:** The Holy See (Vatican City) and the State of Palestine.

Chapter 2: North America

North America is the third-largest continent by area and the fourth-largest by population. In 2026, it remains one of the world's most influential economic zones, driven by the strong trade ties between its three largest nations: Canada, the United States, and Mexico.

Regional Overview: 2026

- **Total Population:** ~621 Million
- **Total Nations:** 3 (Mainland) + 20 (Caribbean and Island Territories)
- **Key Economic Feature:** The **USMCA Review 2026**. This year marks a critical 6-year review of the trade agreement between the U.S., Mexico, and Canada to ensure continued economic cooperation.
- **Climate Trends:** 2026 has seen an early "pollen season" and lengthening growing seasons across the continent due to warming trends.

Country Profile: Canada

Canada is the second-largest country in the world by total area, known for its vast natural resources and diverse landscape.

- **Capital City:** Ottawa
- **Population (2026 Est.):** 40.5 Million
- **Official Languages:** English, French
- **Currency:** Canadian Dollar (CAD)
- **Climate Zone:** Primarily Subarctic and Continental; Oceanic in the west.
- **2026 Key Fact:** Canada continues to see rapid population growth in its urban centers like Toronto and Vancouver, largely driven by its active immigration programs.

Country Profile: United States of America

The United States is the world's largest economy and the third most populous nation.

- **Capital City:** Washington, D.C.
- **Population (2026 Est.):** 348 Million
- **Official Language:** English (Official in 32 states; common nationwide)
- **Currency:** United States Dollar (USD)
- **Climate Zone:** Varied (Humid Continental, Humid Subtropical, Arid, and Marine).
- **2026 Key Fact:** The U.S. is currently navigating a major "Western Hemisphere Pivot," focusing its diplomatic and economic efforts on strengthening ties within the Americas.

Country Profile: Mexico

Mexico is the world's most populous Spanish-speaking country and a global leader in manufacturing.

- **Capital City:** Mexico City
- **Population (2026 Est.):** 132 Million
- **Official Language:** Spanish (and 68 indigenous languages)
- **Currency:** Mexican Peso (MXN)
- **Climate Zone:** Tropical, Arid, and Semi-Arid.

- **2026 Key Fact:** Mexico is now the #1 trading partner of the United States, surpassing China in total goods exchanged, largely due to "nearshoring" trends in the automotive and electronics industries.

Snapshot: Central America & The Caribbean

This region consists of smaller nations acting as a bridge between the two Americas.

- **Major Nations:** Guatemala, Cuba, Haiti, Dominican Republic, and Panama.
- **Key Fact:** The **Panama Canal** remains the most vital maritime shortcut in the world, facilitating global trade between the Atlantic and Pacific oceans.

Canada Feature: Ottawa Parliament Hill

Mexico Feature: Mexico City Skyscrapers

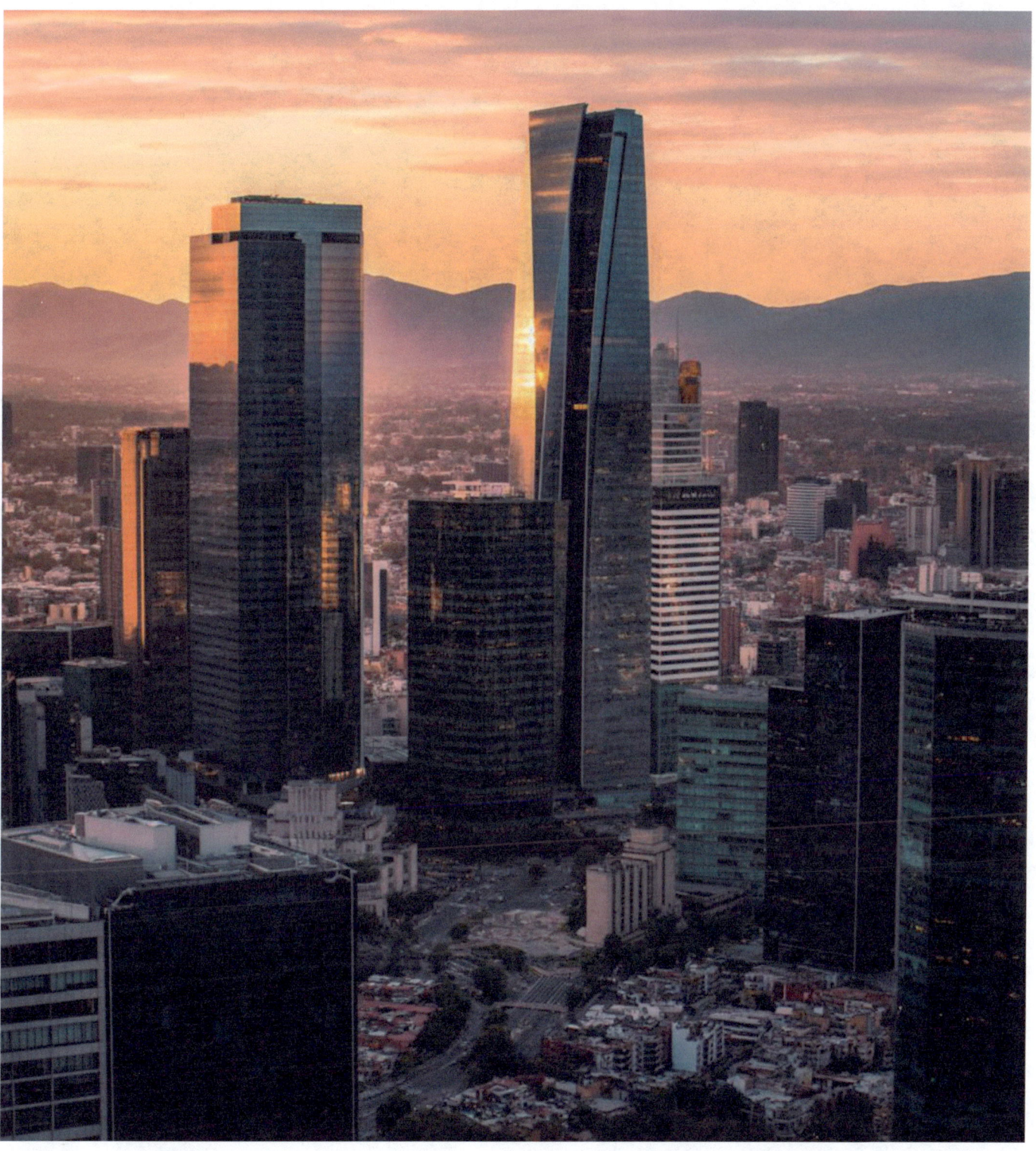

Maritime Trade: Panama Canal

Economic Illustration: USMCA Trade Graphic

Chapter 3: South America

South America is a continent of geographic extremes, home to the world's largest rainforest (the Amazon) and the longest mountain range (the Andes). In 2026, the region is a global leader in renewable energy and agricultural exports.

- **Total Population**: ~445 Million
- **Total Nations:** 12 Sovereign States + 2 Territories (French Guiana and Falkland Islands)
- **Key Economic Feature**: The **Lithium Triangle**. 2026 sees record-high exports from Argentina, Bolivia, and Chile, which together hold the majority of the world's lithium—essential for the global shift to electric vehicles.
- **Climate Trends**: Increased focus on **Amazon Conservation**. In 2026, satellite data shows a significant slowing of deforestation rates as regional pacts for "Bio-Economy" development take hold.

Country Profile: Brazil

Brazil is the largest country in South America and the fifth-largest in the world. It occupies nearly half of the continent's landmass.

- **Capital City:** Brasília
- **Population (2026 Est.):** 213.5 Million
- **Official Language:** Portuguese
- **Currency**: Brazilian Real (BRL)
- **Climate Zone:** Primarily Tropical; Semiarid in the northeast and Temperate in the south.
- **2026 Key Fact:** Brazil has become the world's leading exporter of soybeans and iron ore, while also transitioning its energy grid to over **85% renewable sources**.

Country Profile: Argentina

Argentina is the second-largest nation in South America, stretching from the subtropics to the icy tip of Tierra del Fuego.

- **Capital City:** Buenos Aires
- **Population (2026 Est.):** 46.8 Million
- **Official Language:** Spanish
- **Currency**: Argentine Peso (ARS)
- **Climate Zone:** Varied (Subtropical in the north, Arid in the center, and Cold/Windy in the south).
- **2026 Key Fact:** The Vaca Muerta region has turned Argentina into a major regional energy exporter, significantly stabilizing its trade balance this year.

Country Profile: Colombia

Colombia is the only South American country with coastlines on both the Pacific Ocean and the Caribbean Sea.

- **Capital City:** Bogotá

- **Population (2026 Est.):** 53.1 Million
- **Official Language:** Spanish
- **Currency:** Colombian Peso (COP)
- **Climate Zone:** Tropical along the coasts; Highland (cool/temperate) in the Andes.
- **2026 Key Fact:** Colombia has solidified its position as a global "Coffee Giant" while rapidly expanding its eco-tourism industry, which reached record visitor numbers in early 2026.

Snapshot: The Andean Nations

The Andes Mountains define the geography of the western coast.

- **Major Nations:** Chile, Peru, Ecuador, and Bolivia.
- **Key Fact:** Peru remains the world's second-largest producer of copper. In 2026, new "Green Mining" regulations have been implemented to protect the high-altitude water sources of the Andes.

Environmental Feature: Amazon Rainforest Aerial View

The Lithium Triangle: Salar de Uyuni, Bolivia

Brazil Feature: Christ the Redeemer, Rio de Janeiro

Argentina Feature: Buenos Aires Obelisco

Colombia Feature: Coffee Plantation Landscape

The Andes Feature: Peru Mountain Landscape

Chapter 4: Europe

Europe is the world's second-smallest continent by land area but remains a global powerhouse in terms of economy, history, and international diplomacy. In 2026, the continent is defined by a rapid shift toward digital integration and "Green Energy" self-sufficiency.

Regional Overview: 2026

- **Total Population:** ~742 Million
- **Total Nations:** 44 Sovereign States

- **Key Economic Feature: The Digital Euro.** 2026 marks a significant milestone in the rollout of the European Central Bank's digital currency, aimed at streamlining cross-border payments across the Eurozone.
- **Climate Trends: The Great Heat Adaptation.** Following several record-breaking summers, European cities have implemented massive "Urban Cooling" projects, including vertical gardens and reflectant roofing to combat rising temperatures.

Country Profile: Germany

Germany is the most populous member of the European Union and the continent's largest economy.

- **Capital City:** Berlin
- **Population (2026 Est.):** 84.1 Million
- **Official Language:** German
- **Currency:** Euro (EUR)
- **Climate Zone:** Marine West Coast (temperate/seasonal).
- **2026 Key Fact:** Germany has officially reached its goal of generating over **60% of its electricity from renewable sources,** primarily wind and solar, making it a global leader in the energy transition.

Country Profile: France

France is the largest country in the European Union by land area and a global leader in culture and technology.

- **Capital City:** Paris
- **Population (2026 Est.):** 65.1 Million
- **Official Language:** French
- **Currency:** Euro (EUR)
- **Climate Zone:** Oceanic in the west; Mediterranean in the south.
- **2026 Key Fact:** Following the legacy of the 2024 Olympics, Paris has completed its "15-Minute City" transformation, where residents can reach all essential services within a short walk or bike ride.

Country Profile: United Kingdom

The UK, consisting of England, Scotland, Wales, and Northern Ireland, remains a major global financial hub.

- **Capital City:** London
- **Population (2026 Est.):** 68.3 Million
- **Official Language:** English
- **Currency:** British Pound (GBP)
- **Climate Zone:** Temperate Maritime.

- **2026 Key Fact:** The UK is currently expanding its "Atlantic Declaration" trade partnerships, focusing on high-tech collaboration and AI safety standards with North American partners.

Country Profile: Ukraine

Located in Eastern Europe, Ukraine is a vital agricultural producer and is currently undergoing one of the largest infrastructure reconstruction projects in history.

- **Capital City:** Kyiv
- **Population (2026 Est.):** ~37 Million (Variable due to migration)
- **Official Language:** Ukrainian
- **Currency:** Hryvnia (UAH)
- **Climate Zone:** Temperate Continental.
- **2026 Key Fact:** Ukraine has become a "Digital Laboratory" for Europe, with many of its government services and infrastructure management systems fully digitized and resilient against cyber-threats.

Snapshot: The Nordic Countries

These nations are consistently ranked as the happiest and most stable in the world.

- **Major Nations:** Sweden, Norway, Denmark, Finland, and Iceland.
- **Key Fact:** In 2026, the Nordic region has become the first "Cashless Zone" in the world, with over **98% of all transactions** occurring digitally.

Germany Feature: Brandenburg Gate, Berlin

France Feature: Vertical Gardens in Paris (Urban Cooling)

UK Feature: London Skyline and River Thames

Ukraine Feature: Modern Kyiv Skyline

The Cashless Society: Nordic Digital Payments

Economic Milestone: Digital Euro Illustration

Chapter 5: Asia

Asia is the world's largest and most populous continent, containing roughly **60% of the global population**. In 2026, Asia remains the primary engine of global economic growth, led by massive technological advancements and urban development.

Regional Overview: 2026

- **Total Population:** ~4.8 Billion
- **Total Nations:** 48 Sovereign States
- **Key Economic Feature: The Rise of the "Asian Century."** By 2026, the combined GDP of Asian nations has surpassed that of the rest of the world combined (in terms of Purchasing Power Parity).
- **Climate Trends: Renewable Megaprojects.** Asia is currently home to the world's largest solar and wind farms, particularly in the Gobi Desert and the plains of India, as the region works to balance high energy demand with carbon reduction goals.

Country Profile: India

As of 2026, India is the world's most populous country and one of its fastest-growing major economies.

- **Capital City:** New Delhi
- **Population (2026 Est.):** 1.47 Billion
- **Official Languages:** Hindi, English (plus 21 other scheduled languages)
- **Currency:** Indian Rupee (INR)
- **Climate Zone:** Varied (Tropical Monsoon in the south, Temperate in the north, Arid in the west).
- **2026 Key Fact:** India has become a global "Space Superpower," with its 2026 lunar missions focusing on sustainable moon-base technology and resource mapping.

Country Profile: China

China remains a global leader in manufacturing, technology, and infrastructure, currently focusing on "High-Quality Development."

- **Capital City:** Beijing
- **Population (2026 Est.):** 1.41 Billion
- **Official Language:** Standard Chinese (Mandarin)
- **Currency:** Renminbi (Yuan - CNY)
- **Climate Zone:** Diverse (Subtropical in the south, Arid in the west, Continental in the north).
- **2026 Key Fact:** China is now the world leader in **Autonomous Transport**, with several major cities operating fully driverless public transit networks as of early 2026.

Country Profile: Japan

Japan is an archipelago nation known for its high-tech industry and unique blend of traditional culture and modern innovation.

- **Capital City:** Tokyo
- **Population (2026 Est.):** 122 Million

- **Official Language:** Japanese
- **Currency:** Japanese Yen (JPY)
- **Climate Zone:** Mostly Temperate (Subtropical in the south, Subarctic in the north).
- **2026 Key Fact:** To address its aging population, Japan has integrated "Service Robotics" into nearly every sector of its economy, from healthcare to retail, by 2026.

Country Profile: Indonesia

Indonesia is the world's largest archipelagic state and the most populous country in Southeast Asia.

- **Capital City: Nusantara** (The new capital city on the island of Borneo, officially inaugurated as the seat of government).
- **Population (2026 Est.):** 288 Million
- **Official Language:** Indonesian (Bahasa Indonesia)
- **Currency:** Indonesian Rupiah (IDR)
- **Climate Zone:** Tropical Rainforest.
- **2026 Key Fact:** The move to the new capital, Nusantara, was designed to be a "Smart, Green Forest City," serving as a global model for sustainable urban relocation.

Snapshot: The Middle East (West Asia)

This region is a vital crossroads for global energy and trade.

- **Major Nations:** Saudi Arabia, United Arab Emirates, Iran, Turkey (Türkiye), and Qatar.
- **Key Fact:** In 2026, Saudi Arabia's **"Vision 2030"** projects are reaching major milestones, including the partial opening of **The Line** (a 170km long mirrored skyscraper city), fundamentally changing the geography of the desert

India Feature: Lunar Mission Moon Base Concept

China Feature: Autonomous Public Transit

Japan Feature: Service Robotics in Healthcare

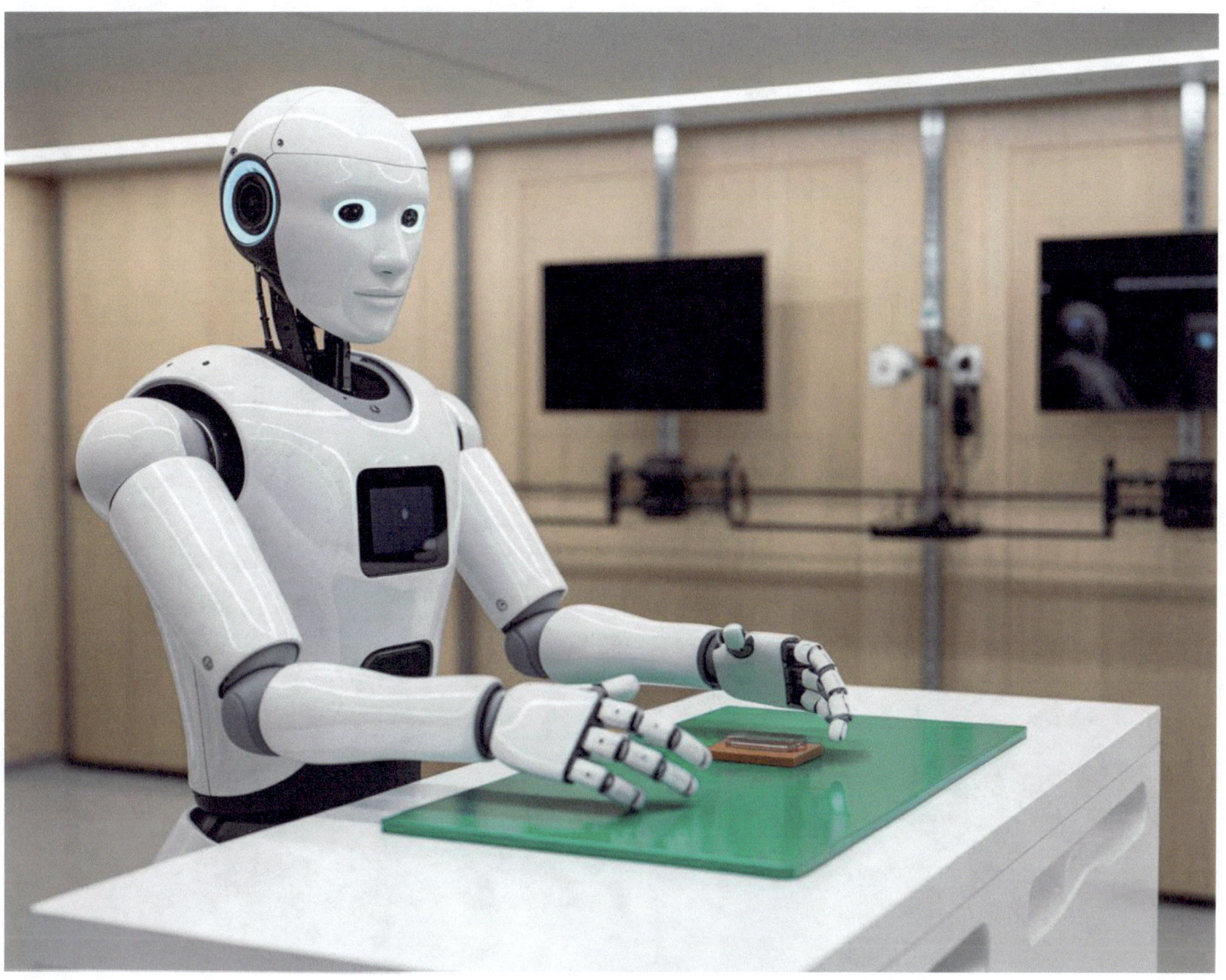

Indonesia Feature: Nusantara "Green Forest City" Design

Middle East Snapshot: The Line, Saudi Arabia Render

Renewable Megaprojects: Gobi Desert Solar Farm

Chapter 6: Africa

Africa is the world's second-largest and second-most populous continent. In 2026, it is recognized as the global leader in demographic growth and digital leapfrogging. With the youngest population on Earth, the continent is rapidly transforming into a massive single market through increased regional cooperation

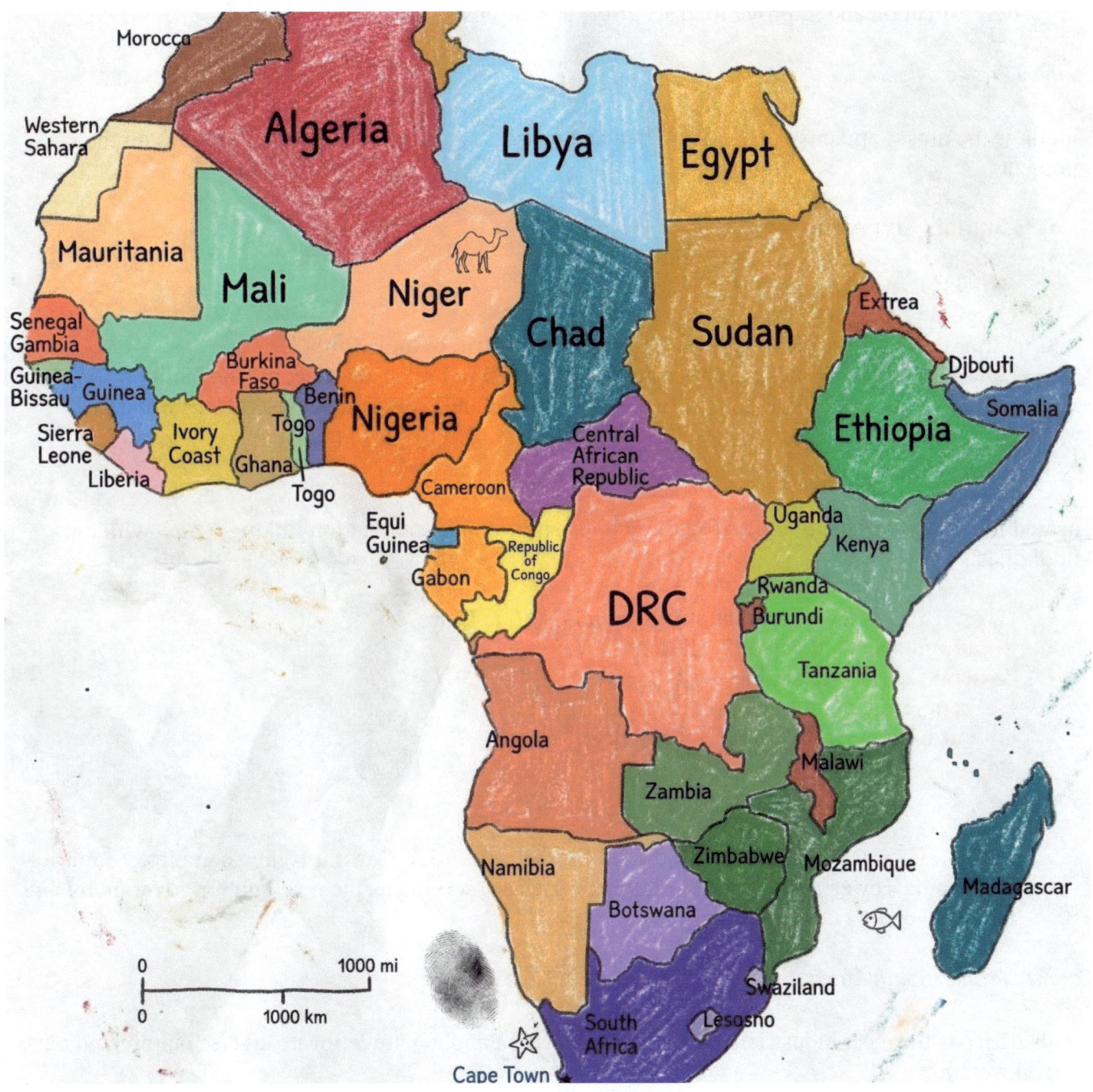

- **Total Population:** ~1.52 Billion
- **Total Nations:** 54 Sovereign States
- **Key Economic Feature: The AfCFTA Milestone.** 2026 marks a turning point for the African Continental Free Trade Area, with intra-African trade reaching record highs as digital payment systems now allow seamless currency exchange across borders.
- **Climate Trends: The Great Green Wall Progress.** Significant reforestation and land restoration milestones have been met this year across the Sahel region, helping to combat desertification and improve food security for millions.

Country Profile: Nigeria

Nigeria is the most populous country in Africa and possesses one of the largest economies on the continent.

- **Capital City:** Abuja
- **Population (2026 Est.):** 242 Million
- **Official Language:** English
- **Currency:** Naira (NGN)
- **Climate Zone:** Tropical (Equatorial in the south, Arid in the north).
- **2026 Key Fact:** Nigeria's tech ecosystem, centered in Lagos, has become the "Silicon Valley of Africa," leading the continent in fintech innovation and cinematic exports (Nollywood).

Country Profile: Egypt

Located in the northeast corner of Africa, Egypt is a transcontinental nation linking Africa with the Middle East.

- **Capital City:** New Administrative Capital (NAC) / Cairo
- **Population (2026 Est.):** 117 Million
- **Official Language:** Arabic
- **Currency:** Egyptian Pound (EGP)
- **Climate Zone:** Arid Desert (Hot and dry).

- **2026 Key Fact:** The transition to the **New Administrative Capital** is now complete, featuring the "Iconic Tower"—the tallest building in Africa—serving as the new hub for government and finance.

Country Profile: South Africa

South Africa is the most industrialized economy in Africa and is known for its diverse culture and vast mineral wealth.

- **Capital Cities**: Pretoria (Executive), Bloemfontein (Judicial), Cape Town (Legislative)
- **Population (2026 Est.):** 61.5 Million
- **Official Languages**: 12 Official Languages (including Zulu, Xhosa, Afrikaans, and English)
- **Currency**: South African Rand (ZAR)
- **Climate Zone**: Mostly Semiarid; Subtropical along the east coast.
- **2026 Key Fact**: South Africa remains a global leader in "Critical Minerals," providing the majority of the world's platinum and manganese required for high-tech manufacturing.

Country Profile: Ethiopia

Ethiopia is the second-most populous nation in Africa and one of the world's fastest-growing economies over the last decade.

- **Capital City:** Addis Ababa
- **Population (2026 Est.):** 138 Million
- **Official Language**: Amharic
- **Currency**: Ethiopian Birr (ETB)
- **Climate Zone**: Tropical Monsoon (with significant highland variations).
- **2026 Key Fact**: The **Grand Ethiopian Renaissance Dam (GERD)** is now fully operational, making Ethiopia the largest exporter of clean hydroelectric power in East Africa.

Snapshot: The East African Federation (EAF)

The East African Community (EAC) continues to move toward closer political and economic integration.

- **Major Nations**: Kenya, Tanzania, Uganda, Rwanda, Burundi, South Sudan, DR Congo, and Somalia.
- **Key Fact**: In 2026, the **East African Shilling** (a proposed common currency) has begun its pilot phase in cross-border trade between Kenya and Tanzania.

Nigeria Feature: Lagos Skyline (Fintech Hub)

Egypt Feature: The New Administrative Capital and Iconic Tower

Ethiopia Feature: The Grand Ethiopian Renaissance Dam (GERD)

South Africa Feature: Cape Town and Table Mountain

Climate Initiative: The Great Green Wall Reforestation

Economic Milestone: AfCFTA Digital Payment Graphic

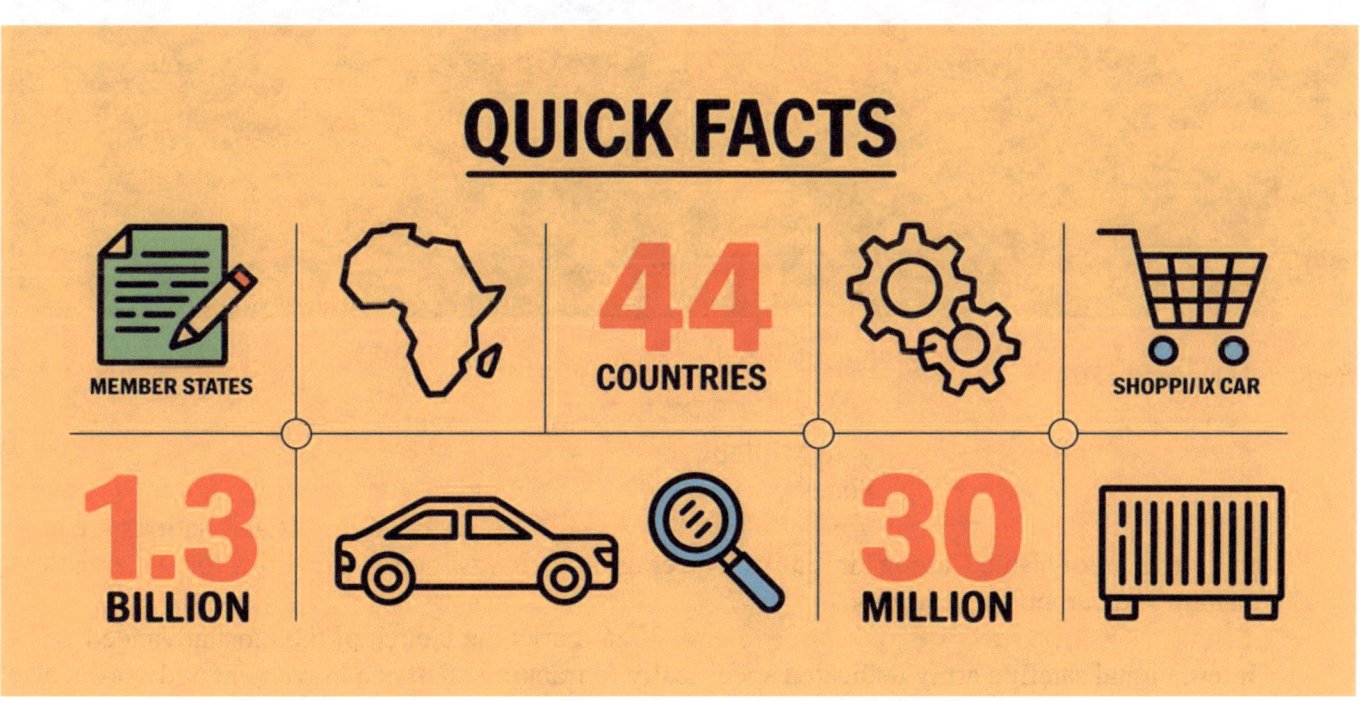

Chapter 7: Oceania & Antarctica

This chapter covers the vast expanse of the Pacific Ocean, including the continent of Australia, the islands of Melanesia, Micronesia, and Polynesia, and the frozen continent of Antarctica.

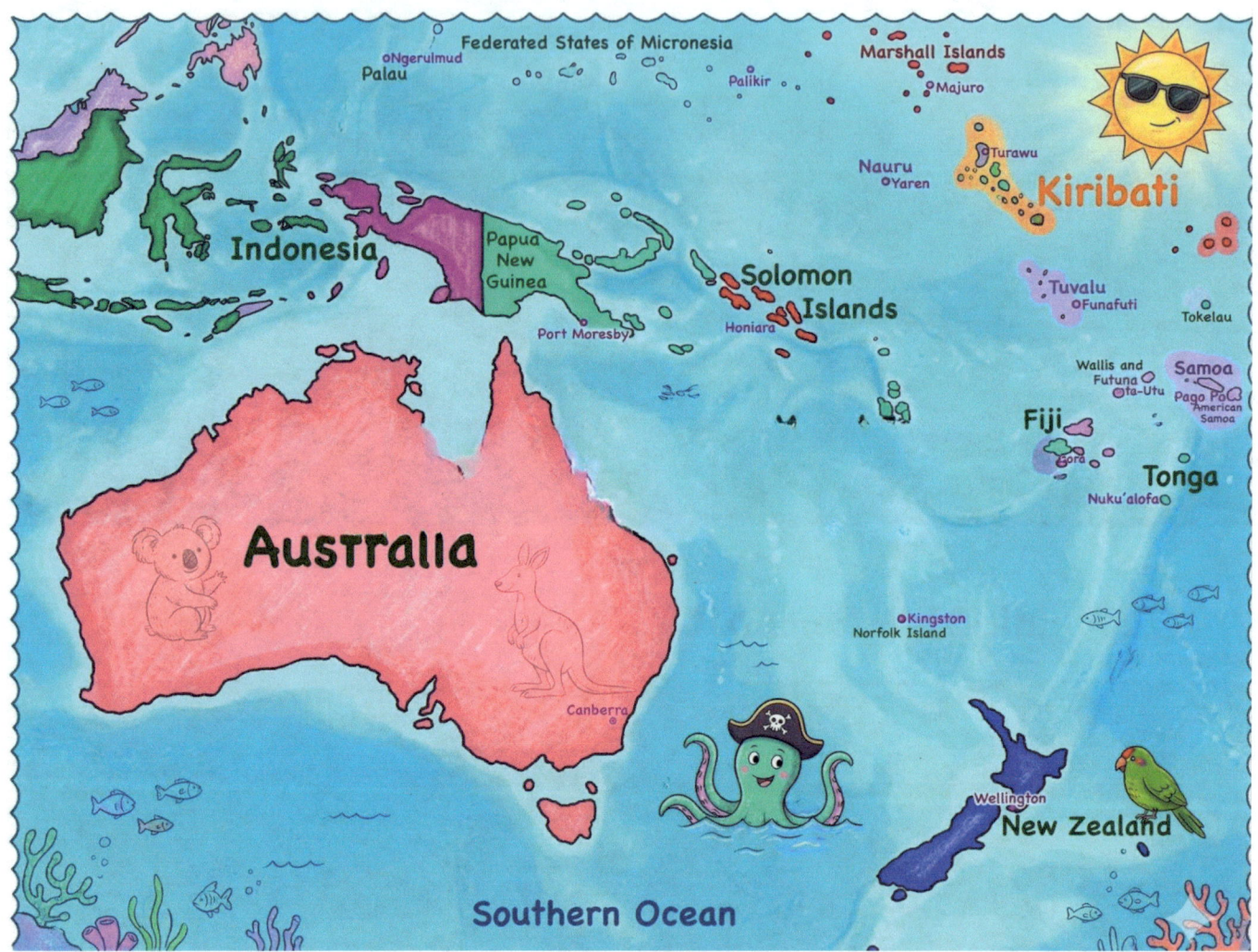

Regional Overview: 2026

- **Total Population (Oceania):** ~46 Million
- **Total Nations:** 14 Sovereign States
- **Key Geopolitical Feature: Blue Economy Leadership.** In 2026, Pacific Island nations are at the forefront of "Blue Carbon" initiatives, leveraging their vast ocean territories for sustainable fishing and carbon sequestration.
- **Climate Trends: Antarctic Ice Monitoring.** 2026 marks the launch of the most advanced international satellite array dedicated specifically to tracking shelf-ice movement and sea-level contributions from the South Pole.

Country Profile: Australia

Australia is the world's largest island and its smallest continent. It is a major global exporter of minerals and agricultural products.

- **Capital City:** Canberra
- **Population (2026 Est.):** 27.2 Million
- **Official Language:** English
- **Currency:** Australian Dollar (AUD)
- **Climate Zone:** Primarily Arid and Semi-Arid; Temperate in the south and east; Tropical in the north.
- **2026 Key Fact:** Australia has become a "Renewable Energy Superpower," exporting liquid hydrogen produced from solar and wind power to markets across Asia.

Country Profile: New Zealand

New Zealand consists of two main islands (North and South) and is renowned for its progressive social policies and stunning natural landscapes.

- **Capital City:** Wellington
- **Population (2026 Est.):** 5.3 Million
- **Official Languages:** English, Māori, NZ Sign Language
- **Currency:** New Zealand Dollar (NZD)
- **Climate Zone:** Temperate Maritime.
- **2026 Key Fact:** In 2026, New Zealand celebrates a major milestone in its "Predator Free 2050" goal, successfully restoring several mainland "islands" of native biodiversity.

Country Profile: Papua New Guinea

Papua New Guinea is one of the most culturally diverse countries in the world, with over 800 indigenous languages spoken.

- **Capital City:** Port Morcsby
- **Population (2026 Est.):** 10.8 Million
- **Official Languages:** Tok Pisin, English, Hiri Motu
- **Currency:** Kina (PGK)
- **Climate Zone:** Tropical.
- **2026 Key Fact:** The country is currently a central hub for "Sustainable Forestry," working with international partners to protect its massive rainforest—the third largest in the world.

Antarctica: The Frozen Continent

Antarctica is the only continent with no permanent human residents and no sovereign government. It is governed by the **Antarctic Treaty System**.

- **Area:** ~14.2 million square kilometers.
- **Population:** Seasonal (Approx. 1,000 in winter to 5,000 in summer, primarily scientists).
- **2026 Key Fact:** The **Ross Sea Marine Protected Area**—the world's largest—has seen a significant recovery in toothfish and krill populations this year, proving the success of large-scale maritime conservation.

Snapshot: Small Island Developing States (SIDS)

These nations are the most vulnerable to climate change but lead the world in environmental advocacy.

- **Major Nations:** Fiji, Samoa, Solomon Islands, Vanuatu, and Kiribati.
- **Key Fact:** In 2026, **Fiji** has become a regional hub for "Digital Nomads," offering specialized visas for remote workers to help diversify its tourism-dependent economy.

Australia Feature: Sydney Skyline and Opera House

New Zealand Feature: Milford Sound Landscape

Papua New Guinea Feature: Rainforest Aerial View

Antarctica Feature: Ice Shelf and Research Station

Pacific Islands Snapshot: Fiji Tropical Coastline

Blue Economy Concept: Ocean Conservation Visual

Chapter 8: Global Flags and National Symbols

Flags and national symbols are more than just designs; they represent the history, values, and identity of a nation. In 2026, these symbols continue to evolve as countries update their visual identities to reflect modern aspirations.

The Purpose of National Symbols

National symbols serve three primary functions:

1. **Unity:** Providing a common visual point for citizens.
2. **Recognition:** Allowing for instant identification in international diplomacy and sports.
3. **Heritage:** Distilling centuries of history into colors and shapes.

Key Flag Designs and Their Meanings

While every flag is unique, many share common themes based on regional history or shared values.

Design Type	Common Meaning	Examples
Tricolors	Often represent Liberty, Equality, and Fraternity.	France, Italy, Germany
Stars & Crescents	Traditionally associated with Islamic heritage or guidance.	Türkiye, Pakistan, Malaysia
Southern Cross	Represents a location in the Southern Hemisphere.	Australia, New Zealand, Brazil
Pan-African Colors	Red (blood), Gold (wealth), and Green (land).	Ethiopia, Ghana, Senegal

Recent Changes and Updates (As of 2026)

Several nations have recently updated or refined their symbols to better reflect their contemporary status:

- **Kyrgyzstan (Update):** In late 2023/early 2024, the sun rays on the national flag were straightened to look more like a sun and less like a flower, symbolizing a more "radiant" and "direct" future for the nation.
- **Honduras (Color Shift):** The blue in the Honduran flag was officially shifted to a brighter "Turquoise" to distinguish it from other Central American flags and celebrate its Caribbean coastline.
- **The Move Toward Inclusivity:** Many nations have updated their **National Coats of Arms** in 2025 and 2026 to include indigenous symbols alongside colonial or post-colonial imagery.

Identifying World Flags: A Quick Guide

For easy reference, most world flags can be categorized by their dominant layout:

1. **Horizontal Stripes:** (e.g., Germany, Russia, Gabon) - The most common layout.
2. **Vertical Stripes:** (e.g., France, Nigeria, Belgium) - Often associated with republican movements.
3. **Canton Flags:** (e.g., USA, Greece, Malaysia) - Feature a distinct design in the top-left corner.
4. **Unique Shapes: Nepal** remains the only sovereign nation with a non-rectangular flag (two stacked triangles).

- **National Anthems:** Musical representations of a country's spirit.
- **National Animals/Birds:** Used to symbolize strength (e.g., the Bald Eagle for the USA) or uniqueness (e.g., the Kiwi for New Zealand).
- **National Flowers:** Often used in diplomacy and branding (e.g., the Cherry Blossom for Japan).

Update Spotlight: Kyrgyzstan's New Sun Ray Design

Update Spotlight: Honduras Turquoise Flag

Unique Shapes: The Flag of Nepal

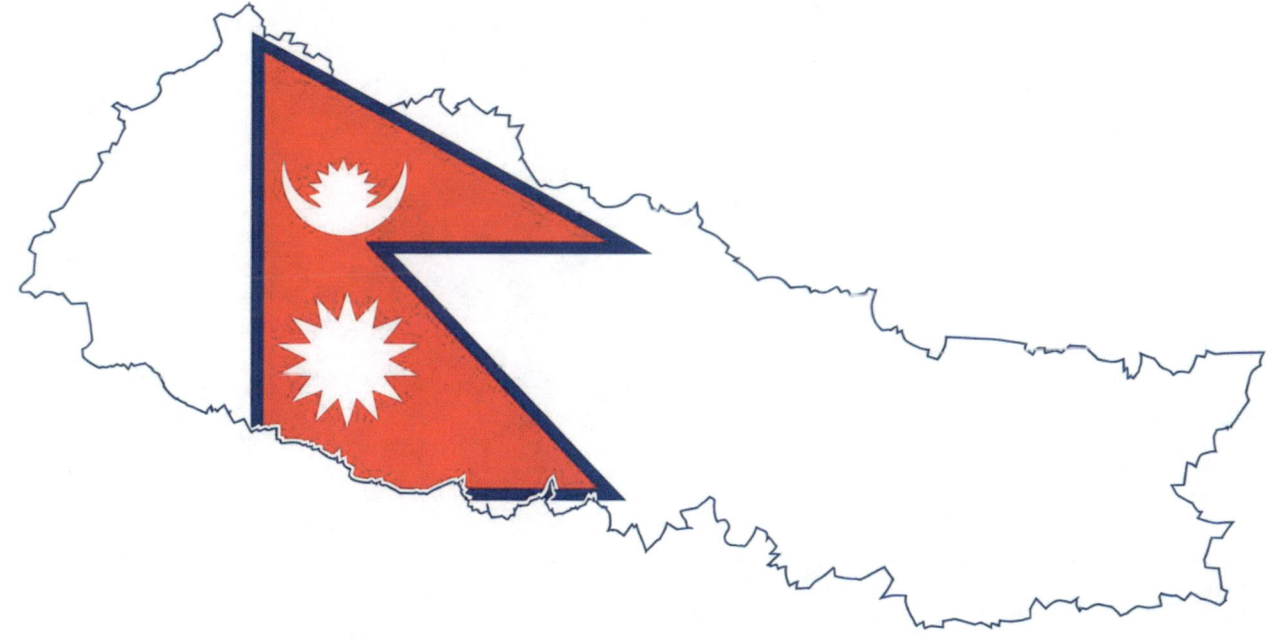

National Symbols: Animals and Flowers Montage

Chapter 9: World Capitals and Major Cities Directory

A capital city is more than just a seat of government; it is often the cultural and economic heart of a nation. As of 2026, several nations have completed the transition to new, purpose-built capitals designed for the modern era.

The Role of a Capital City

- **Administrative Hub:** The location of the national parliament, supreme court, and head of state.
- **Diplomatic Center:** The primary site for foreign embassies and international negotiations.
- **Symbolic Value:** Representing the identity and future ambitions of the people.

Recent Capital City Changes (2024–2026)

One of the most significant trends in 2026 geography is the "Relocation Movement," where countries move their capitals to alleviate overcrowding or centralize administration.

Country	Previous Capital	Current Capital (2026)	Reason for Change
Indonesia	Jakarta	**Nusantara**	Sinking land and overcrowding in Jakarta.
Egypt	Cairo	**New Administrative Capital**	Centralizing government in a "Smart City" hub.
Equatorial Guinea	Malabo	**Ciudad de la Paz**	Moving the capital to a more central, mainland location.

Major Global Megacities

In 2026, "Megacities"—defined as metropolitan areas with more than **10 million people**—continue to grow. Here are the most significant urban hubs by region:

- **Asia:** Tokyo (Japan) remains the largest, followed closely by Delhi (India) and Shanghai (China).
- **Africa:** Lagos (Nigeria) and Kinshasa (DRC) are the fastest-growing cities on the continent.
- **The Americas:** Mexico City, São Paulo, and New York City remain the dominant economic engines.

- **Europe**: Istanbul (Turkey), Moscow (Russia), and London (UK) hold the highest urban populations.

Global Capitals Directory (A–Z Highlights)

- **Afghanistan:** Kabul
- **Albania:** Tirana
- **Algeria:** Algiers
- **Andorra:** Andorra la Vella
- **Angola:** Luanda
- **Argentina:** Buenos Aires
- **Australia:** Canberra
- **Austria:** Vienna
- **Bahamas:** Nassau
- **Bangladesh:** Dhaka
- **Belgium:** Brussels
- **Brazil:** Brasília
- **Canada:** Ottawa
- **China:** Beijing
- **Denmark:** Copenhagen
- **Ethiopia:** Addis Ababa
- **France:** Paris
- **Germany:** Berlin
- **India:** New Delhi
- **Japan:** Tokyo
- **Nigeria:** Abuja
- **United Kingdom:** London
- **United States:** Washington, D.C.

Snapshot: "The Twin Cities"

Some countries utilize more than one capital to balance power between different branches of government or regions.

- **South Africa**: Pretoria (Executive), Bloemfontein (Judicial), and Cape Town (Legislative).
- **Bolivia**: Sucre (Constitutional) and La Paz (Administrative).
- **Netherlands**: Amsterdam (Constitutional) and The Hague (Seat of Government).

The Relocation Movement: Nusantara, Indonesia

The Smart City Hub: Egypt's New Administrative Capital

Global Megacity (Asia): Tokyo Shinjuku Skyline

Global Megacity (Africa): Lagos Island Skyline

The Twin Cities: Cape Town, South Africa

High-Altitude Administration: La Paz, Bolivia

Chapter 10: Geography Fact Sheets: Mountains, Rivers, and Oceans

The physical features of the Earth define our borders, influence our climates, and dictate where we live. This chapter provides a high-level summary of the "giants" of our planet as they are measured and monitored in 2026.

The World's Highest Peaks

Mountains act as "water towers" for the planet, storing freshwater in glaciers that feed the world's major rivers.

Rank	Mountain	Range	Elevation	Location
1	Mount Everest	Himalayas	8,848.86 m	Nepal / China
2	K2	Karakoram	8,611 m	Pakistan / China
3	Kangchenjunga	Himalayas	8,586 m	Nepal / India
4	Lhotse	Himalayas	8,516 m	Nepal / China
5	Makalu	Himalayas	8,485 m	Nepal / China

- **2026 Key Fact:** Advances in satellite GPS technology in early 2026 have allowed for even more precise monitoring of Everest's height, which continues to change slightly due to tectonic activity.

The World's Longest Rivers

Rivers are the lifelines of civilizations. The debate between the Nile and the Amazon for the title of "Longest River" continues, but most cartographers use the following standard measurements.

1. **The Nile (Africa):** ~6,650 km. It flows through 11 countries and is the primary water source for Egypt and Sudan.
2. **The Amazon (South America):** ~6,400 km. It carries the largest volume of water in the world and sustains the Amazon Rainforest.

3. **The Yangtze (Asia):** ~6,300 km. The longest river in Asia, flowing entirely within China.
4. **Mississippi-Missouri (North America):** ~6,275 km. The largest river system in North America.
5. **Yenisei (Asia):** ~5,539 km. The largest river system flowing into the Arctic Ocean.

The Great Oceans and Seas

Oceans cover approximately **71% of the Earth's surface**. In 2026, the health of these oceans is a primary focus of international law.

- **The Pacific Ocean:** The largest and deepest. It is home to the **Mariana Trench,** which reaches a depth of ~10,935 meters.
- **The Atlantic Ocean:** The second-largest, currently seeing increased shipping traffic due to new "Green Maritime Corridors."
- **The Indian Ocean:** The warmest ocean, vital for global trade routes between Asia and Africa.
- **The Southern Ocean:** Officially recognized as the fifth ocean, it plays a critical role in regulating global climate by circulating cold water.
- **The Arctic Ocean:** The smallest ocean. In 2026, it is being monitored closely as ice-free summer periods become more frequent, opening new potential trade routes.

Snapshot: Iconic Landforms

- **The Sahara Desert (Africa):** The world's largest hot desert, roughly the size of the United States.
- **The Great Barrier Reef (Oceania):** The largest living structure on Earth, visible from space.
- **The Caspian Sea (Asia/Europe):** The world's largest inland body of water (actually a salt lake).

Highest Peaks: Mount Everest

Longest Rivers: The Amazon River

Ocean Spotlight: The Southern Ocean

Iconic Landforms: The Sahara Desert

Iconic Landforms: The Great Barrier Reef

Chapter 11: 2026 Climate Zones and Environmental Data

Understanding our planet's climate is essential for navigating the changes we see today. In **early 2026**, the global community is focused on climate resilience—the ability to adapt to a warming world while protecting our natural resources.

The Köppen-Geiger Climate System

This atlas uses the **Köppen-Geiger classification,** the gold standard for climatology in 2026. It categorizes the world into five main zones:

1. **Tropical (Group A):** Hot and humid, found near the equator (e.g., Brazil, Indonesia, Nigeria).
2. **Dry (Group B):** Areas with very little rainfall, including deserts and steppes (e.g., Saudi Arabia, Sahara, Outback Australia).
3. **Temperate (Group C):** Warm summers and mild winters (e.g., Mediterranean, Southeastern USA, Eastern China).
4. **Continental (Group D):** Large temperature swings between hot summers and freezing winters (e.g., Russia, Canada, Northern USA).
5. **Polar (Group E):** Constantly cold, with average temperatures below **10°C** even in summer (e.g., Antarctica, Greenland).

2026 Global Climate Snapshot

- **Temperature Update:** February 2026 was recorded as the **fifth-warmest February** in history.
- **The 1.5°C Threshold:** 2026 reports show that global temperatures are frequently hovering near the **1.5°C warming threshold** compared to pre-industrial levels, increasing the frequency of "extreme weather events."
- **Ocean State:** As of March 2026, the **La Niña** weather pattern is dissipating. Scientists are monitoring a transition toward a "neutral" state, with early signs of a potential **El Niño** shift by late 2026.

Major Environmental Milestones of 2026

This year is a historic one for environmental protection:

- **The High Seas Treaty (January 17, 2026):** This landmark agreement officially entered into force, establishing the first-ever international framework to protect biodiversity in the "High Seas" (waters beyond national borders).
- **International Year of Rangelands and Pastoralists:** 2026 has been designated by the United Nations to raise awareness about sustainable land practices in the world's grasslands and the livelihoods of those who depend on them.
- **Urban Greening:** Major cities like **Tashkent** and **Nusantara** are leading the "Green Space" movement in 2026, aiming to increase urban tree cover to 30% to combat the "Urban Heat Island" effect.

1. **Water Scarcity:** Over **2 billion people** live in countries experiencing high water stress as of 2026.
2. **Ice Loss:** Arctic sea ice extent continues to trend below average, with 2026 seeing some of the lowest levels recorded for the winter season.
3. **Biodiversity Loss:** International summits in 2026 (like COP17 in Armenia) are focused on protecting the "Lithium Triangle" and Amazon rainforest from industrial degradation.

Climate Snapshot: 1.5°C Threshold Infographic

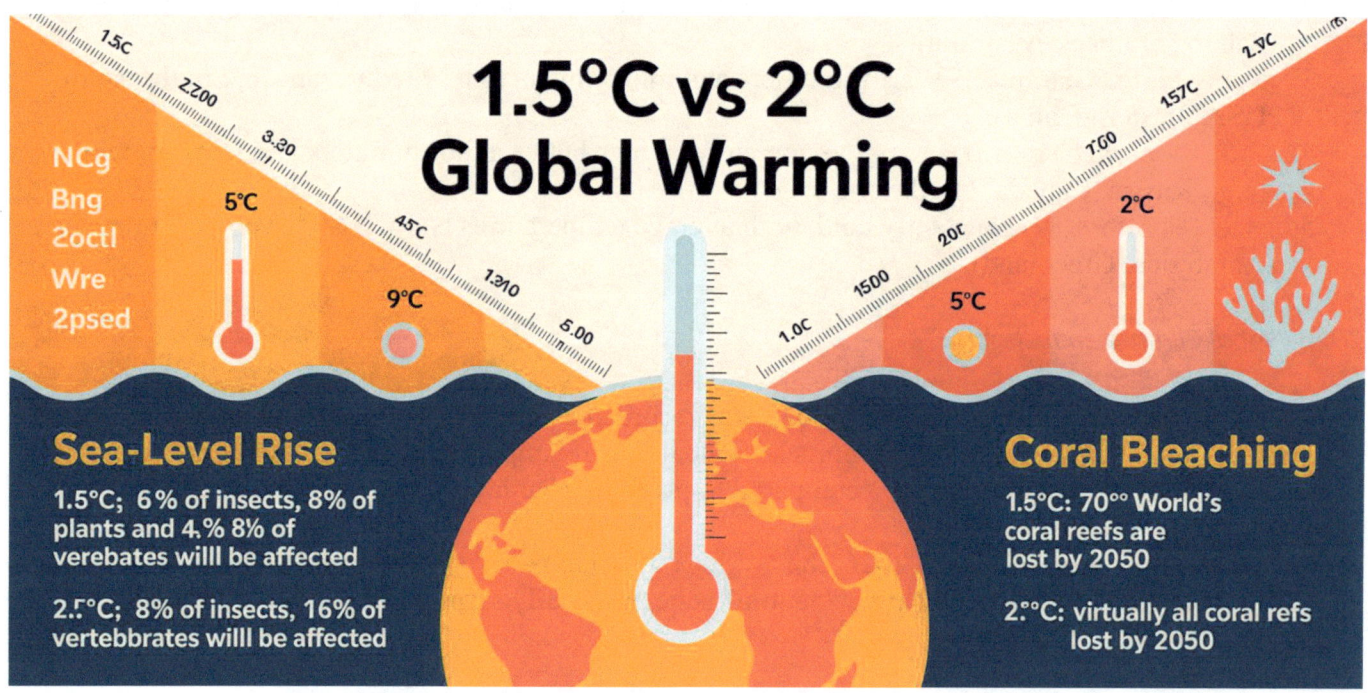

Urban Greening: Nusantara Sustainable Design

Ocean Conservation: High Seas Treaty Graphic

Chapter 12: Socio-Economic Rankings (2026)

This final chapter provides a data-driven snapshot of the world in **2026**. These rankings help illustrate the shifting balance of economic power and the progress of human development across the globe.

Top 10 Economies by Nominal GDP (2026 Projections)

Gross Domestic Product (GDP) measures the total value of goods and services produced. A major milestone in 2026 is **India officially overtaking Japan** to become the world's 4th largest economy.

Rank	Country	Projected GDP (2026)	2026 Growth Rate
1	United States	$31.82 Trillion	2.1%
2	China	$20.65 Trillion	4.2%
3	Germany	$5.33 Trillion	0.9%
4	India	$4.51 Trillion	6.2%
5	Japan	$4.46 Trillion	0.6%
6	United Kingdom	$4.23 Trillion	1.3%
7	France	$3.56 Trillion	0.9%
8	Italy	$2.70 Trillion	0.8%
9	Russia	$2.51 Trillion	1.0%

Rank	Country	Projected GDP (2026)	2026 Growth Rate
10	Canada	$2.42 Trillion	1.5%

Global Literacy & Education (2026 Status)

Literacy is the foundation of economic growth. By 2026, the global adult literacy rate has climbed to approximately **87%**.

- **Universal Literacy (100%):** Nations like **Andorra, Finland, Norway, and Uzbekistan** maintain near-perfect literacy rates through consistent investment in mandatory education.
- **Rapid Climbers:** Countries in Southeast Asia (like **Vietnam**) and East Africa (like **Rwanda**) have seen the fastest literacy gains in the 2024–2026 period due to digital learning initiatives.
- **The Literacy Gap:** Sub-Saharan Africa and parts of South Asia still face challenges, with some nations reporting rates below 50% due to regional instability and lack of infrastructure.

Human Development Index (HDI) Leaders

The HDI measures more than just money; it combines **life expectancy, education, and income per capita**.

1. **Iceland** (Ranked #1 in 2026)
2. **Norway**
3. **Switzerland**
4. **Denmark**
5. **Germany**

Appendix: 2026 Glossary of Geographical Terms

- **Archipelago:** A group or chain of islands (e.g., Indonesia, Japan).
- **Biome:** A large naturally occurring community of flora and fauna (e.g., Tundra, Tropical Rainforest).
- **GDP (Nominal):** The market value of all final goods and services from a nation in a given year.
- **Isthmus:** A narrow strip of land with sea on either side, forming a link between two larger areas of land (e.g., Panama).
- **Sovereign State:** A political entity that has a permanent population, defined borders, and the power to govern itself.

Index of Countries and Territories

(Sample for Large Print Layout)

- **A:** Afghanistan (95), Algeria (66), Argentina (31), Australia (72)
- **B:** Brazil (30), Belgium (44), Bangladesh (51)
- **C:** Canada (24), China (52), Colombia (32)
- **D–E:** Denmark (45), Egypt (67), Ethiopia (68)
- **F–G:** France (43), Germany (42), Ghana (69)
- **I–J:** India (50), Indonesia (53), Italy (46), Japan (54)
- **N–U:** Nigeria (65), United Kingdom (44), United States (25)

Made in the USA
Monee, IL
06 April 2026

47835171R10042